Pupil Book 4

Spelling

Author: Chris Whitney

William Collins' dream of knowledge for all began with the publication of his first book in 1819. A self-educated mill worker, he not only enriched millions of lives, but also founded a flourishing publishing house. Today, staying true to this spirit, Collins books are packed with inspiration, innovation and practical expertise. They place you at the centre of a world of possibility and give you exactly what you need to explore it.

Collins. Freedom to teach.

Published by Collins
An imprint of HarperCollins*Publishers*
The News Building
1 London Bridge Street
London
SE1 9GF

Browse the complete Collins catalogue at
www.collins.co.uk

© HarperCollins*Publishers* Limited 2015

10 9 8 7 6 5 4 3 2 1

ISBN 978-0-00-813339-9

British Library Cataloguing in Publication Data
A Catalogue record for this publication is available from the British Library

Edited by Jessica Marshall
Cover design and artwork by Amparo Barrera
Internal design concept by Amparo Barrera
Typesetting by Jouve India Private Ltd
Illustrations by Aptara and QBS

Printed in Italy by Grafica Veneta S.p.A.

Pupil Book 4
Spelling

Contents

Adding suffixes beginning with vowels to words of more than one syllable

A suffix is a group of letters added to the end of a root word. When you add a suffix starting with a vowel to a word of more than one syllable, the spelling rule depends on whether the last syllable is stressed or not. If the last syllable is stressed, double the final consonant. For example: **gar**den + **er** = garde**ner**, but be**gin** + **er** = begi**nn**er.

Get started

Copy and complete the chart by sorting these words into two groups. One has been done for you.

1. garden

2. listen

3. water

4. begin

5. prefer

6. forget

7. answer

Consonant not doubled	Consonant doubled
garden	

Try these

Copy and complete the table by adding suffixes to these words.
One has been done for you.

Root word	-ed	-ing
wonder	*wondered*	
regret		
prefer		
offer		

Now try these

Add **-er, -d** or **-ing** to each of these words and then use them
in sentences of your own.

1. enrol
2. forbid
3. target
4. limit
5. commit
6. cancel
7. admit
8. visit

The /i/ sound spelled y

Remember, there are some words in which the **/i/** sound is spelled as a letter **y**. For example, the **y** in g**y**m sounds like the **i** in r**i**m. Here are some other words that follow this pattern: m**y**th, p**y**ramid, m**y**stery.

Get started

Copy and complete the words by adding the missing letter, **i** or **y**. The first one has been done for you.

1. p_ramid

   Answer: *pyramid*

2. s_lly

3. g_m

4. cr_stal

5. s_mptom

6. pr_nce

7. m_stery

8. thr_lling

Try these

Copy these sentences and correct the incorrectly spelled words. The first one has been done for you.

1. Nayati enjoyed visiting the piramids and would remember them forever.

   Answer: *Nayati enjoyed visiting the pyramids and would remember them forever.*

2. The photos were amazing – now I want to go to Egipt too!

3. This rainy weather is tipical in winter!

4. The music club's simbol is a violin.

5. My Uncle Jim often tells us some very misterious stories!

6. The fluffy young cignets will turn into elegant swans.

7. Frankie had learned the lirics to his favourite song.

8. The gimnast did a flip and landed on her feet.

Now try these

Correct the spelling of these words and use them in sentences of your own.

1. sillable
2. rhithm
3. phisical
4. cimbal
5. histerical
6. sistem
4. oxigen
8. himn

The /u/ sound spelled ou

In some words, the letters **ou** are pronounced as if they were a **u**. For example, the **ou** in t**ou**ch sounds like the **u** in m**u**ch.

Get started

Copy these sentences and label them 'correct' or 'incorrect' to show whether the underlined word has been spelled correctly. The first one has been done for you.

1. *Chrissie needed <u>courage</u> to go and see the dentist. correct*

2. I have always been good friends with my <u>cusin</u>.

3. Cary waved the brush and finished his painting with a <u>flourish</u>.

4. Tariq plays the <u>troumpet</u> in the school band.

5. Bea <u>jumped</u> over the puddle.

6. Miss Freeman said Louis was looking very <u>scruffy</u>.

7. Lia borrowed Katka's <u>hairbroush</u> without asking.

8. That maths test was really <u>tugh</u>.

Try these

Copy these sentences and correct the incorrectly spelled words. The first one has been done for you.

1. Grandad hasn't planted enugh tomatoes.

   Answer: *Grandad hasn't planted <u>enough</u> tomatoes.*

2. Are you sure you have enugh time to clean up before Mum comes back?

3. Mr Godwin always encurages us to enjoy science.

4. Rajesh saw a cuple of robins nesting in the tree.

5. Kerry has a lot of truble learning her spellings.

6. It's tugh work climbing hills!

7. Zahra's cookery teacher said it was important to be well nurished.

8. You can look at the paintings but you can't tuch them.

Now try these

Correct the spelling of these words and use them in sentences of your own.

1. flurish
2. cuple
3. nurish
4. curage
5. cusin
6. duble
7. rugh
8. enugh

The prefixes dis- and mis-

A prefix is a group of letters that you can add to the start of a root word. The prefix **dis-** normally means 'not'. For example: **dis- + agree = disagree**

The prefix **mis-** normally means 'badly' or 'incorrectly'. For example: **mis- + spell = misspell**

Sometimes we use the prefixes **dis-** and **mis-** when there is not a clear root word.

Get started

Look at these pairs of words. Copy out the word from each pair that has the correct prefix. The first one has been done for you.

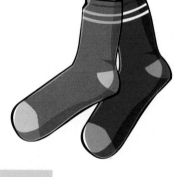

1. mismatched / dismatched: *mismatched*

2. misagree / disagree

3. misspell / disspell

4. misshape / disshape

5. miscourage / discourage

6. misobey / disobey

7. misbehave / disbehave

8. misgraceful / disgraceful

Try these

Add the correct prefix, **dis-** or **mis-**, to each of these root words and write the new word. The first one has been done for you.

1. ____conduct

   Answer: *misconduct*

2. ____honest

3. ____approval

4. ____guided

5. ____connect

6. ____judge

7. ____understand

8. ____like

Now try these

Add the correct prefix, **dis-** or **mis-**, to each word. Then use it in a sentence of your own.

1. similar

2. agree

3. matched

4. calculated

5. judge

6. satisfied

7. understood

8. loyal

The prefixes in-, ir-, im- and il-

The prefix **in-** is used to mean 'not'. When you add **in-** to a root word, you do not change the spelling of the root word. But sometimes you do have to change the spelling of **in-**.

If you add **in-** to a root word beginning with **r**, **in-** becomes **ir-**. For example: **ir** / responsible

If you add **in-** to a root word beginning with **m** or **p**, **in-** becomes **im-**. For example: **im** / possible

If you add **in-** to a root word beginning with **l**, **in-** becomes **il-**. For example: **il** / logical

Get started

Copy the words below, separating the prefix and root word. One has been done for you.

1. irresistible

   Answer: *ir / resistible*

2. independent

3. indefinitely

4. irreplaceable

5. illegal

6. irregular

7. immortal

8. incorrect

Try these

Copy and complete the words with the correct prefix, **in-**, **ir-**, **im-** or **il-**. One has been done for you.

1. ____credible

   Answer: *incredible*

2. ____considerate

3. ____resistible

4. ____mobile

5. ____ability

6. ____literate

7. ____practical

8. ____describable

Now try these

Use the words below in sentences of your own. One has been done for you.

improbable, immeasurable, irreplaceable, independent, inability, illegible, immobile, inescapable

Answer: *It is <u>improbable</u> that you will see a monkey riding on a crocodile.*

The prefixes re- and inter-

The prefix **re-** means 'again'. The prefix **inter-** means 'between' or 'among'. When you add **re-** or **inter-** to a word, you do not have to make any changes to the root word.

For example: **inter** / national, **re** / discover

Get started

Add the prefix **re-** or **inter-** to each word and write the new word. One has been done for you.

1. ____route

   Answer: *reroute*

2. ____departmental

3. ____interpret

4. ____call

5. ____consider

6. ____adjust

7. ____related

8. ____build

Try these

Write a short definition for each word. Use a dictionary if you need to. One has been done for you.

1. rewrite: *to write something again*

2. react:

3. readjust:

4. redial:

5. international:

6. rearrange:

7. interact:

8. interchangeable:

Now try these

Use the words below in sentences of your own. One has been done for you.

reread, rewrap, rewind, relive, intermingle, intermission, intersection, interview

Answer: *Jacob has <u>reread</u> his favourite book five times.*

17

The prefixes sub- and super-

The prefix **sub-** means 'under' or 'less than'. The prefix **super-** means 'above' or 'more than'. When you add **sub-** or **super-** to a root word, you do not change the spelling of the root word.

For example: **super**/visor, **sub**/way

Get started

Write these words, splitting the word into its prefix and root word. One has been done for you.

1. supermarket

   Answer: *super / market*

2. subdivide

3. subsection

4. superheated

5. subordinate

6. subclass

7. superbug

8. supercharge

Try these

Add the prefix **sub-** or **super-** to these root words and write the new word. One has been done for you.

1. ____market

   Answer: *supermarket*

2. ____impose

3. ____marine

4. ____merge

5. ____standard

6. ____continent

7. ____tropical

8. ____heated

Now try these

Use the words below in sentences of your own. One has been done for you.

subsection, supermarket, superstar, subheading, submarine, subcontract, submerge, superglue

Answer: *The newspaper had many different <u>subsections</u>.*

The prefixes anti- and auto-

The prefix **anti-** is used to mean 'against'. The prefix **auto-** is used to mean 'self' or 'own'.

For example: **anti**biotics, **auto**graph

Get started

Write these words, splitting the word into its prefix and root word. One has been done for you.

1. automobile

   Answer: *auto / mobile*

2. antioxidants

3. antiglare

4. antithesis

5. autograph

6. autopilot

7. autodidact

8. autotimer

Try these

Add the prefix **anti-** or **auto-** to these root words and write the new word. One has been done for you.

1. ____septic

   Answer: *antiseptic*

2. ____mobile

3. ____biography

4. ____dote

5. ____matter

6. ____bacterial

7. ____viral

8. ____body

Now try these

Use the words below in sentences of your own. One has been done for you.

antiseptic, antidote, autopilot, automaton, anticlimax, autograph, antihero, antisocial

Answer: *Emma cleaned her graze with antiseptic lotion.*

The suffix –ation

The suffix **-ation** turns verbs into nouns.
For example: inform = inform**ation**

If the verb ends in an **e**, remove the **e** before
adding **-ation**.
For example: aspire = aspir**ation**

Get started

Identify the verbs from the nouns below and write out the verbs.
One has been done for you.

    1. alteration

        Answer: *alter*

    2. confrontation

    3. temptation

    4. condensation

    5. accusation

    6. sensation

    7. preservation

    8. reputation

Try these

Choose the correct spelling for each word. Then write the word.
One has been done for you.

1. determination / determineation

   Answer: *determination*

2. compilation / compileation

3. reformtion / reformation

4. converseation / conversation

5. determination / determineation

6. infestation / infesteation

7. obligiation / obligation

8. coliniseation / colonisation

Now try these

Use these words in sentences of your own.
One has been done for you.

condensation, alteration, frustration,
temptation, information, composition,
decomposition, inclination

Answer: *The windows were wet from*
condensation.

The suffix –ly

You can turn an adjective into an adverb by adding the suffix **-ly**.
For example: final + **ly** = final**ly**

However, if the root word has more than one syllable and ends in **y**, you change the **y** to an **i**.
For example: pretty + **ly** = prett**ily**

If the root word ends with **–le**, change the **–le** to **–ly**.
For example: simple + **ly** = simp**ly**

If the root word ends with **ic**, add **-ally** instead of **-ly**.
For example: basic + **ally** = basic**ally**

A few words do not fit the rules – these have to be remembered.
For example: **truly**, **wholly**

Get started

Add the suffix **-ally** or **-ly** to the following words and copy them into the correct column. One has been done for you.

1. comic		**2.** humble	
3. able		**4.** historic	
5. critic		**6.** scribble	
7. logic		**8.** terrible	

Words ending in –ally	Words ending in –ly
comically	

Try these

Change the adjective into an adverb by adding the correct suffix. The first one has been done for you.

1. energetic

   Answer: *energetically*

2. heroic

3. usual

4. happy

5. poetic

6. noble

7. greedy

Now try these

Use five of the following words in five sentences of your own. One has been done for you.

brightly, skilfully, sumptuously, happily, frantically, truly, wholly, realistically

Answer: *The sun shone <u>brightly</u>.*

The pattern -sure as in measure

The **/sher/** sound at the ends of words is spelled **-sure**.

The spelling pattern **-sure** can make two different sounds. For example, **/zher/** as in mea**sure** and **/sher/** as in as**sure**.

Get started

Copy and complete the table to sort these into two groups: words spelled correctly and words spelled incorrectly. One has been done for you.

1. pleasure

2. reasure

3. assure

4. enclozure

5. sure

6. composhure

7. leisure

8. discomposuore

Correct	Incorrect
pleasure	

Try these

Put the letters in the correct order to spell each word. Then write the word. One has been done for you.

1. crmupoeos

Answer: *composure*

2. eislersdpua

3. eatrresu

4. csloiuders

5. eulrsie

6. xesrpeuo

7. rsausree

8. fosoeurercl

Now try these

Use these words in sentences of your own. One has been done for you.

enclosure, displeasure, pleasure, composure, closure, exposure, treasure, assure

Answer: *The children looked at the chickens in their wire <u>enclosure</u>.*

The endings -ture and -cher

Words that end with a **/cher/** sound often have the letter pattern **-ture**.

For example: crea**ture**

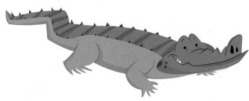

But remember, some words are spelt exactly as they sound.

Get started

Copy and complete the table to sort these words into two groups according to how the **/cher/** sound is spelled: **-ture** or **-cher**.

1. adventure
2. pasture
3. agriculture
4. richer
5. signature
6. gesture
7. catcher
8. departure

-ture	-cher
adventure	

Try these

Choose from the two word endings and copy out the correct word. One has been done for you.

1. texture / texcher

   Answer: *texture*

2. architecture / architeccher

3. watcher / wature

4. leccher / lecture

5. pitcher / piture

6. feacher / feature

7. streture / stretcher

8. nurcher / nurture

Now try these

Use the words below in sentences of your own. One has been done for you.

agriculture, departure, fracture, vulture, gesture, future, sculpture, tincture

Answer: <u>*Agriculture*</u> *is the science or practice of farming.*

The ending -sion

The **/shun/** sound at the end of words can often be spelled **-sion**.

For example: confu**sion**

Get started

Find the spelling mistakes in each word and write the word correctly. One has been done for you.

1. revizion

Answer: *revision*

2. illushun

3. excurtion

4. comprehention

5. immershun

6. verzion

7. repultsion

8. averzion

Try these

Words with **–sion** at the end are nouns. Copy and complete the table to match the nouns to their related verbs. One has been done for you.

Noun	Verb
conclusion	tense
television	*conclude*
erosion	extend
tension	explode
extension	televise
explosion	apprehend
implosion	erode
apprehension	implode

Now try these

Use these words in sentences of your own. One has been done for you.

television, diversion, pension, explosion, erosion, expansion, expulsion, mansion

Answer: *Aggie settled down to watch some television.*

31

The suffix -ous

Many adjectives end with the suffix **-ous**. Add the suffix **-ous** to the end of the root word.

If the root word ends with **e**, like fam**e**, you normally drop the **e** before adding **-ous**. For example: fam**ous**

If the root word ends with a soft **/g/** sound, like courage, you keep the final **e**. For example: courage**ous**

If the root word ends with **y**, like vary, you change **y** to **i** before adding **-ous**. For example: vari**ous**

If the root word end with **-our**, like glam**our**, you change **-our** to **-or** before adding the **-ous**.
For example: glam**our** = glamor**ous**

Sometimes there is not a clear root word.
For example: obvi**ous**

If there is an **/ee/** sound before the **-ous,** it is normally spelled with an **i**. For example: env**ious**. However, sometimes this **/ee/** sound is spelled with an **e**. For example: spontan**eous**

However, there are exceptions to these rules.

Get started

Identify and write the root word of each adjective. One has been done for you.

1. ridiculous   Answer: *ridicule*   **2.** humorous

3. miraculous   **4.** envious

5. vigorous   **6.** prosperous

7. hazardous   **8.** famous

Try these

Find the spelling mistakes in each word and write the word correctly. One has been done for you.

1. adventureous

   Answer: *adventurous*

2. spontanyous

3. spaceious

4. jealious

5. numarous

6. humourous

7. outragouse

8. mischievius

Now try these

Use these words in sentences of your own. One has been done for you.

famous, nauseous, contagious, obvious, generous, momentous, mischievous, anonymous

Answer: *Adjay's virus was contagious, so the doctor told him to stay in bed.*

The endings -tion, -sion, -ssion and -cian

There are different ways of spelling the **/shun/** sound: **-tion**, **-ssion**, **-sion** and **-cian**.

The most common way of spelling the **/shun/** sound is **-tion**. Use this when the root word ends in **-t** or **-te**. For example: inject = injec**tion**. If the root word ends in **-te** drop the final **-e** before adding **-ion**. For example: comple**te** = comple**tion**

For root words ending in **-ss** or **-mit**, spell the **/shun/** sound **-ssion**.

For root words ending in **-d** or a consonant then **-se**, spell the **/shun/** sound **-sion**. If the root word ends in **-d**, like exten**d**, drop the **-d** before adding **-sion**.

For root words ending in **-c** or **-s**, spell the **/shun/** sound **-cian**. If the root word ends in **-cs**, drop the final **s** before adding **-ian**.

Get started

Choose the suffix that makes the spelling correct for each word. Then write the correct word. One has been done for you.

1. temptation / temptassion / temptasion

   Answer: *temptation*

2. completion / complession / complecian

3. examination / examinassion / examininacian

4. examinasion / examination / examinassion

5. vertion / verssion / version

Try these

Add the **/shun/** endings to these root words and write them out. One has been done for you.

1. confess

   Answer: *confession*

2. pollute

3. except

4. electric

5. admit

6. comprehend

7. mathematics

8. submit

Now try these

Use these words in sentences of your own. One has been done for you.

vacation, fiction, mission, excursion, diversion, fraction, obsession, magician

Answer: *This year we went camping for our* <u>*vacation*</u>.

The /k/ sound spelled ch

Remember, there are some words where the /k/ sound is spelled **ch**. For example, the **ch** in monarch sounds like the **k** in banker. These words often came originally from Greek.

Get started

Copy and complete the table to sort these words into two groups: words where the /k/ sound is spelled **ch** and words where it is not. One has been done for you.

1. monarch
2. punch
3. anchor
4. chemistry
5. bleach
6. character
7. chalk
8. flinch

The /k/ sound spelled ch	The /k/ sound not spelled ch
monarch	

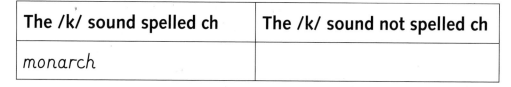

Try these

Fill in each gap with the letters **ch** or **c**. Then write the word.
One has been done for you.

1. _aos

   Answer: *chaos*

2. ba_ing

3. or_ estra

4. S_otland

5. te_nology

6. e_o

7. s_ary

8. stoma_

Now try these

Correct the spellings of these words and use them in sentences
of your own. One has been done for you.

1. kord

   Answer: *Charlie strummed a <u>chord</u>*
   on her guitar.

2. kemist

3. kemistry

4. ankor

5. kaos

6. skeme

7. teknical

The /sh/ sound spelled ch

In most words, the **/sh/** sound is spelled with the letters **sh** as in **sh**ower.

However, in some words the **/sh/** sound is spelled with the letters **ch** as in **ch**ef.

Get started

Find the spelling mistake in each word and write it correctly. One has been done for you.

1. shefs

　　Answer: *chefs*

2. shicane

3. shateau

4. quishe

5. shauffeur

6. croshet

7. sashet

8. shaperone

Try these

Put the letters in the correct order to spell each word. Then write the word. One has been done for you.

1. hctue

   Answer: *chute*

2. ousmtache

3. nmaechi

4. echandlier

5. lcathe

6. acuratphe

7. uhicqe

8. eicnh

Now try these

Use these words in sentences of your own. One has been done for you.

machines, brochure, chandelier, parachute, chauffeur, quiche, nonchalant, ricochet

Answer: *Computers are very useful <u>machines</u>.*

The /k/ sound spelled –que and the /g/ sound spelled –gue

In some words, the /k/ sound is spelled **–que**. For example: barbe**que**. In some words, the /g/ sound is spelled **–gue**. For example: ro**gue**

Get started

Find the spelling mistake in each word, then write it correctly. One has been done for you.

1. boutigue

   Answer: *boutique*

2. antigue

3. cataloque

4. vaque

5. fatique

6. grotesgue

7. tonque

8. merinque

Try these

Copy the sentences adding a word from the box below to fill the gaps. One has been done for you.

colleague	intrigue	opaque	plague	physique

1. My _____ was on holiday last week.

   Answer: My <u>colleague</u> was on holiday last week.

2. The athlete trained hard to keep his _____ in good shape.

3. The plot of his latest story was full of mystery _____.

4. Many of the villages were struck down with the _____ and died.

5. The windows in the room were made of _____ glass.

Now try these

Use these words in sentences of your own. One has been done for you.

league, dialogue, intrigue, boutique, grotesque, rogue, colleague, opaque

Answer: One day, John and Casper hoped to play in the big <u>league</u>.

The /s/ sound spelled sc

There are several words in English where the **/s/** sound is spelled **sc**. For example: **sc**ent

Get started

Each gap represents an **/s/** sound. Write the words, correctly filling the gaps with the letters **s** or **sc**. One has been done for you.

1. deci_ion

   Answer: *decision*

2. __ene

3. de__end

4. pre__ent

5. __enery

6. citru__

7. __ience

8. __ocial

Try these

Find the spelling mistakes in the words below and copy them correctly. One has been done for you.

1. seenic

   Answer: *scenic*

2. cresent

3. desent

4. senscible

5. balanse

6. scolid

Now try these

Use these words in sentences of your own. One has been done for you.

scent, discipline, descend, adolescent, fascinate, ascend, scissors

Answer: *The dog picked up the <u>scent</u> of the buried treasure.*

The /ay/ sound spelled ei, eigh and ey

There are lots of different ways of spelling the **/ay/** sound including these three spelling patterns: **ei**, **eigh** and **ey**.

For example:

- v**ei**n
- w**eigh**
- conv**ey**

Get started

Write the letters in the correct order to spell each word. One has been done for you.

1. engih

   Answer: *neigh*

2. vonecy

3. geionruhb

4. eigfn

5. ehisk

6. beiasl

7. egry

8. bbogisleh

Try these

Copy and complete the sentences by choosing the correct spelling of each word. One has been done for you.

1. Tracey chose _____ shoes for the party.
   (beigh / beige / beyge)

   Answer: *Tracey chose <u>beige</u> shoes for the party.*

2. The horses in the stable _____.
   (neyd / nejd / neighed)

3. The good dog always _____ his master.
   (obeighed / obeid / obeyed)

4. There are many _____ in Lapland.
   (reighndeer / reindeer / reyndeer)

5. When it snows, I play on my _____. (sley / sleigh / slei)

6. Jack was learning to _____. (abseil / abseyl / abseighl)

7. We use birthday cards to _____ our greetings.
   (convei / conveigh / convey)

8. Her face was hidden by her bridal _____.
   (veil / veighl / veyl)

Now try these

Use these words in sentences of your own. One has been done for you.

neighbour, beige, survey, volley, reign, veil, weigh, weightlifter

Answer: *Beth's <u>neighbour</u> Chris is really good at football.*

The possessive apostrophe with plural words

A possessive apostrophe shows that something belongs to a person or a thing.

If the person or thing is singular, add an apostrophe + **s**. For example: the girl'**s** bedroom = the bedroom of one girl.

If the person or thing is plural, ending in -**s**, then just add an apostrophe. For example: the girls' bedroom = the bedroom of more than one girl.

If the plural form of the thing does not end with an -**s**, add an apostrophe + **s**. For example: the children's bedroom = the bedroom of the children.

If the singular form of the person or thing ends in -**s**, add an apostrophe + **s**. For example: Louis'**s** bedroom = the bedroom of Louis / the class'**s** books = the books of the class

Get started

Copy and complete the table to sort these words into singular (one) or plural (more than one). One has been done for you.

1. horses'   2. lion's

3. class's   4. actresses'

5. hero's   6. children's

Singular	Plural
	horses'

Try these

Copy each sentence, choosing the correct word to complete it.
One has been done for you.

1. The _____ whistles were loud. (policemen's / policemens')

   Answer: *The <u>policemen's</u> whistles were loud.*

2. The _____ cheese was hard. (mouse's / mouses')

3. All the _____ in the water were green. (boat's / boats')

4. The _____ conductor was ready. (choirs' / choir's)

5. _____ friends were coming for tea. (Bess's / Besses')

6. The _____ dinner was in his bowl. (dogs' / dog's)

7. One _____ shoes were missing. (boy's / boys')

8. The _____ supper was ready. (childrens' / children's)

Now try these

Write the following phrases with the possessive apostrophe.
One has been done for you.

1. The manes that belong to the lions.

   Answer: *the lions' manes*

2. The sails that belong to the ships.

3. The bats that belong to the people.

4. The phones that belong to the man.

5. The sweets that belong to Sandeep.

6. The fields that belong to the farmers.

Homophones and near-homophones (I)

Homophones are words that sound the same but they are spelt differently and have different meanings.

For example: **air** and **heir**

Get started

Choose and write the correct meaning for each word. One has been done for you.

accept	except	bury	affect	meddle
	whether	berry	medal	

1. apart from

    Answer: *except*

2. if

3. alter

4. a small juicy fruit

5. agree to

6. interfere

7. put in the ground

8. an award

Try these

Copy out the sentences, choosing the correct word to complete each one. One has been done for you.

1. Serena walked to the front of the hall to _____ her prize. (accept / except)

   Answer: *Serena walked to the front of the hall to* <u>*accept*</u> *her prize.*

2. The bird ate the _____ from the bush. (buries / berries)

3. The _____ had started to clear up, so Kamal decided to go out. (whether / weather)

4. Mrs Jones, _____ dog was lost, always hoped he'd return. (whose / who's)

5. Samantha's sister told her not to _____ with her jewellery. (medal / meddle)

6. The recent bad weather _____ the harvest. (affected / effected)

7. The athlete was awarded a gold _____. (medal / meddle)

8. The film had excellent special _____. (affects / effects)

Now try these

Use these words in sentences of your own. One has been done for you.

except, accept, bury, medal, effect, weather, who's, meddle

Answer: *Taylor disliked all sports* <u>*except*</u> *football.*

Homophones and near homophones (2)

Homophones are words that sound the same but they are spelt differently and have different meanings.

Get started

Choose and write the correct meaning for each word.

grown	he'll	great	knot	groan
	grate	heal		here

1. to have become larger

   Answer: *grown*

2. he will

3. shred

4. moan

5. in this place

6. to tie or tangle

7. to make well again

8. really good

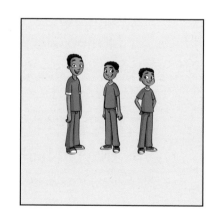

Try these

Copy out the sentences, choosing the correct word to complete each one. The first one has been done for you.

1. Charlie's grandmother said, "You've groan / grown!"

   Answer: *Charlie's grandmother said "You've grown!"*

2. "There are spaces over here / hear," said Julie.

3. If he puts his coat on, heel / he'll feel much warmer.

4. Marek wished she had knot / not eaten all the sweets.

5. Everyone thought the disco was great / grate.

6. The new trainers caused blisters on her heel / heal.

7. At dawn you can hear / here the birds start to sing.

8. I like to great / grate cheese on top of my spaghetti.

Now try these

Use these words in sentences of your own. One has been done for you.

not, groan, hear, knot, grate, he'll, heal, grown

Answer: *Janet wished she had __not__ left her hat unguarded.*

51

Homophones and near-homophones (3)

Homophones are words that sound the same but they are spelled differently and have different meanings.

Get started

Choose and write the correct meaning for each word. One has been done for you.

mist	plane	mane	meat	fair
	peace	fare		meet

1. aeroplane

   Answer: *plane*

2. encounter

3. light fog

4. calm, not fighting

5. long fur around an animal's head

6. food made from animals

7. free from dishonesty

8. the cost of a journey

Try these

Copy out the sentences, choosing the correct word to complete each one. One has been done for you.

1. The weather forecast was for _____ on the hills. (mist / missed)

   Answer: *The weather forecast was for mist on the hills.*

2. Jake _____ his friend now that he was gone. (mist / missed)

3. Lucas liked his biscuits _____, without chocolate. (plane / plain)

4. "Would you like a _____ of cake?" asked Peyton. (piece / peace)

5. The _____ meal was to be eaten at 12pm. (mane / main)

6. I plan to _____ my friend at 3pm, today. (meat / meet)

7. The bus _____ to town costs 60p. (fare / fair)

8. As the last children left, there was _____ again. (piece / peace)

Now try these

Use these words in sentences of your own. One has been done for you.

mane, mist, plane, peace, meat, fair, fare, plain

Answer: *The lion's <u>mane</u> was long and thick.*

Homophones and near homophones (4)

Homophones are words that sound the same but they are spelled differently and have different meanings.

Get started

Choose and write the correct meaning for each word. One has been done for you.

bawl	brake	male	seen
reign	rain	ball	scene

1. to slow down or stop

   Answer: *brake*

2. cry or shout loudly

3. not female

4. looked at

5. rule as king or queen

6. water falling from the sky

7. used in various sports

8. a section of a play

Try these

Copy out the sentences, choosing the correct word to complete each one. One has been done for you.

1. The burglar had to _____ the window to get in. (brake / break)

   Answer: *The burglar had to <u>break</u> the window to get in.*

2. The tennis _____ crossed the line. (ball / bawl)

3. The old man _____ in his mule. (reined / reigned)

4. The postman delivered my _____ on time this morning. (mail / male)

5. The _____ needed more rehearsal. (scene / seen)

6. Our Queen has _____ for over 60 years. (rained / reigned)

7. _____ has fallen in the valleys today. (Rein / Rain / Reign)

8. I have _____ lightning in the sky tonight. (scene / seen)

Now try these

Use these words in sentences of your own. One has been done for you.

seen, brake, bawl, male, rein, scene, mail, break

Answer: *Sabir had <u>seen</u> the whole match.*